# FUNERALS

# FUNERALS
## CHURCHLEADERS
### PASTORAL POCKET GUIDES

First Edition: Year 2022
Funerals (ChurchLeaders Pastoral Pocket Guides) / Outreach, Inc.
Paperback ISBN: : 978-1-958585-89-4
eBook ISBN: 978-1-958585-88-7

**CHURCHLEADERS**
PRESS

*Colorado Springs*

CHURCHLEADERS
PASTORAL POCKET GUIDES

# FUNERALS

*Written by*
Mikal Keefer

*General Editor*
Matt Lockhart

**CHURCHLEADERS**
PRESS

*Colorado Springs*

# Contents

*ChurchLeaders Pastoral Pocket Guides Introduction*    5

**Getting Started**
1. Welcome to the Funerals Pocket Guide    7

**The Basics**
2. The Basics Aren't So Basic Anymore    9
3. Do This Now    13
4. Before the Funeral    20
5. During the Viewing    32
6. During the Funeral    34
7. After the Funeral    41

**Helpful Tools**
8. Scriptures That Comfort and Encourage    44
9. Sample Sermons    52
10. Prayers to Share    67
11. Self-Care    70
12. Pro Tips    73

*About the Contributors*    78

## ChurchLeaders
## Pastoral Pocket Guides Introduction

*Be shepherds of God's flock that is under your care, watching over them—not because you must, but because you are willing, as God wants you to be; not pursuing dishonest gain, but eager to serve; not lording it over those entrusted to you, but being examples to the flock.*
(1 Peter 5:2-3)

The work of a shepherd is never done. One minute you're preparing a sermon and the next you're making an emergency hospital visit or planning an unexpected funeral.

When called to your common and recurring ministerial duties (such as hospital visits, weddings, baptisms, and funerals, to name a few) where do you turn for practical advice or just a couple fresh ideas?

You could spend hours online, scrolling through dozens of sites, or pull that thick, old minister's manual off your shelf. Now you can turn to these new **Pastoral Pocket Guides**, designed especially for busy pastors like you. They're quick reads, each book laser-focused on a specific area of ministry. Packed with practical

guidance, tips, and tools, they'll help make taking care
of your flock a little easier.

Thank you for being a willing shepherd. May God
bless and guide you in your ministry!

—**Matthew Lockhart,** General Editor

# 1 WELCOME TO THE FUNERALS POCKET GUIDE

*A* youth group member carelessly changes lanes while driving home from a date. An elderly congregant finally succumbs to cancer. That new baby you welcomed into your church just last month becomes the victim of sudden infant death syndrome.

Within hours, your phone rings and a sad, trembling voice asks: "Will you officiate the funeral?"

"Sure," you say. "Of course."

Then you hang up the phone and do…what?

What comes next?

With this book in hand, you'll know. It's packed with practical advice from pastors who've answered hundreds of those calls. They walk you through how to lead grieving families through the funeral process. They tell you what to do…and not do. What to say… and not say.

And they help you minister effectively in a time when emotions are raw, doubts loom large, and you may find yourself grieving too.

Make no mistake about it—while funerals may not be your favorite ministry activity, few ministry moments have a greater impact.

That's because the death of a loved one shakes us to the core. People standing next to the casket or urn of a loved one are seldom more open to the comfort Christ can offer. And they're seldom in greater need of help as they struggle to make sense of their loss.

Those in grief need you…and your Savior.

As a pastor or church leader, you'll carry the hope of Christ into rooms where hope has all but flickered and died. You'll speak words of life in the very presence of death. You'll offer a gentle touch, a reassuring word, a steady reminder of God's presence and truth.

Leading funerals is a privilege, honor, and part of your calling as you serve your church and community.

But it's also emotionally and spiritually draining. Especially if you're officiating the funeral of a friend, long-time church member, child, or non-believer, you may find yourself conflicted or exhausted.

The wise counsel in this book equips you to bring comfort and share God's truth with hurting hearts, including your own.

# 2 THE BASICS AREN'T SO BASIC ANYMORE

*N*ot so long ago, you knew what to expect at a funeral.

A body was prepared and put on display at a funeral home or church building. Black-clad mourners gathered for music, a sermon, scripture reading, and a slow procession to the graveside of the dearly departed. Then it was back to the church basement for a meal.

Well, that was then and this is now.

Things have changed in the funeral industry, and people like you—church leaders who officiate funerals—are being impacted by those changes.

## Cremation has taken the lead

According to the National Funeral Directors Association, as of 2020, an estimated 56 percent of funerals involved cremation rather than casketed burial.[1] That means the timing of a funeral—often a week or less after a death—has been extended almost indefinitely.

---

1   https://www.rochesterfirst.com/news/funeral-homes-adjust-as-more-americans-choose-cremations-over-burials

No longer are most families constrained by a tight timeline. They can wait for weeks to schedule a funeral or memorial service. The impact of grief remains, but the stress of pulling together a funeral in a few days has abated.

Which is both good…and bad.

Good in that having time to make decisions and gather more family members together can be healing. And bad in that funeral or memorial services are often an emotional "before and after" event.

Before the funeral, the death of a loved one feels fresh and current. But after the funeral, after mourners disperse and life falls back into a steady rhythm, the work of healing usually begins in earnest. Delaying the funeral may delay the healing.

### New options are emerging

Some approaches to dealing with a body are actually *shortening* the amount of time families have to plan a funeral.

A growing trend is "green funerals," which involve placing an unembalmed body into a biodegradable container and burying it directly in the ground.[2] For several reasons, this requires a funeral sooner rather than later.

---

2  https://www.lhlic.com/consumer-resources/green-burial

Also necessitating fast action are "home funerals," where families prepare bodies for burial. Though relatively rare, this cost-saving option is growing in popularity. If you're asked to officiate these sorts of funerals, you'll need to be ready in 24 to 48 hours.

## Funerals have gotten...creative

As cremation has become popular, more funerals are taking place in unconventional locations. The cremains (ashes) of an avid hiker are carried to a favorite overlook and tossed into the wind. Or scattered throughout a park, at the beach, anywhere it's legal, and occasionally where it's not.

Cremains are mixed with tattoo ink and become custom tattoos honoring the deceased, loaded into live ammunition so a 21-shotgun salute can literally send the deceased out with a bang, or pressed into a vinyl album of the deceased's favorite music.

Courtesy of Elysium Space, a portion of cremains can be launched into earth's orbit, where they'll circle the planet for two years and then re-enter the atmosphere as a shooting star.

But no matter how odd the venue or distracting the theatrics, the basics remain: Someone has died, people are mourning, and you're present to share the hope that's in Jesus.

So don't be thrown when someone asks you to officiate a funeral at a roller rink, pub, or halfway up a mountain. Simply adapt the tips you'll find in this book and roll with it.

# 3 DO THIS NOW

*Y*ou'll be better prepared to officiate and serve at your next funeral if you do these seven things before a funeral sits on your schedule:

## 1. Understand Your Role

When you agree to officiate a funeral, what exactly have you agreed to do?

Each funeral is different. One family will ask you to deliver a brief message during the funeral service and a prayer at the graveside. Another family may want you to organize the funeral service, coordinating with a funeral director.

Seldom are you expected to do more than deliver a message and lead in prayer. Funeral directors generally handle everything else.

But you won't know the scope of what you're expected to do until you ask.

So…ask.

Ask the family what they'd like you to do and ask the funeral director the same question. If possible, arrange a time for you, a family representative, and the funeral director to discuss who'll do what and when.

Don't shoulder any responsibility the funeral director is prepared to handle. They're the experts when it comes to funeral logistics and details. You want to own the opportunities that let you minister to those who are hurting, which means shaping the messages shared in the service and at the graveside, selecting appropriate Scripture, and leading in prayer. The rest you can leave to the funeral director.

Your role is to provide pastoral care, so stay focused on doing what you're there to do:

### You're there to provide comfort

Your words are important, but many family members won't remember a word you say at a loved one's funeral; they're too emotionally spent or lost in grief.

But they will remember your presence and that you listened as they poured out their grief, anger, or sadness.

So listen as well as speak. Be a safe place for tears to well up. Be a shoulder to cry on. Be a steady, reassuring port in the storm.

And—here's a tip—carry a few small packets of facial tissues in a pocket. You'll be distributing them to mourners.

### You're there to focus on relationships

Especially with families with no church connection, your presence makes you the de facto family chaplain. You may be called again when another funeral is needed or family members want a pastor for any other reason.

So be intentional about connecting with each family member.

A good place for this to happen is at a viewing of the body prior to the funeral. The funeral itself is usually too hectic to find time with each family member, but viewings are less busy.

Introduce yourself and get the names of family members. Give your card to receptive family members should they wish to talk further, and briefly pray for or with each person.

Jot down names and family relationships as soon as you're alone. Calling people by their names later at the funeral will signal your sincere concern for them.

God often uses relational bridges you build to draw family members closer to himself as they choose to follow up with you or begin attending your church.

### You're there to represent Jesus

Certain words will have an impact, but they often aren't your words; they're Scripture.

God's Word *always* has an impact, even if you can't immediately see it. Become familiar with the passages listed in Chapter 8 and be ready to share them when appropriate. Few mourners want to hear a sermon, but it's a blessing to be reminded that God is aware of their sorrow and loves them.

### You're there to serve

Funerals give you endless opportunities to be kind and compassionate, so approach funerals prayerfully.

Ask God to soften your heart toward that angry widower, the bored niece taking selfies at the graveside, the pallbearer who keeps checking his watch to see if he'll miss kickoff.

How would God have you care for those people? Whose shoulder would God have you place a caring hand on? Who seems lost in thought, unable to make eye contact?

Every funeral you officiate is a short-term mission trip; how does God want to use you as you wade into a family culture that's different from your own?

Pray—continually—as you engage.

### You're not there to have all the answers

Don't let anyone cast you in the role of "Ultimate Answer Person."

You'll hear the question, "Why?" and won't know the answer.

You'll hear "How long will this hurt?" and won't know that answer either.

It's okay not to have all the answers. It's not okay to pretend you do and offer false hope or assurances.

Stick to proclaiming the hope we have in Christ and admit the truth: Some questions have been asked for centuries, and we simply don't have satisfying answers.

We don't know why good people suffer and die or how long their loss will hollow out our lives. But we do know that God is good and he's calling us to trust him. As hard as it is to accept that, it's where we'll find the peace that passes understanding.

## 2. Assemble your team

Wait. *You're* officiating the funeral, right? So…what team?

Keep reading and you'll find out.

But here's the point: connecting with them now when no funeral is scheduled in two days will make the next funeral far easier to navigate.

## 3. Meet local funeral directors

Unless you're in a large city, just a handful of funeral homes are serving your community.

Reach out and meet with their funeral directors in their places of business. Introduce yourself and inquire how they go about serving families. Ask for a tour of their facilities' public areas. Ask what they wish pastors like you knew when it comes to working with them.

Few pastors or church leaders do this, and that's an oversight. A relationship with funeral directors will be invaluable when a parishioner calls to tell you a funeral is needed.

## 4. Chat with your kitchen chief and church janitor

If your church has a kitchen, who's in charge of making things happen there?

Should a family wish to have a reception meal in your facility, who'll set up the room and handle clean-up? Most churches have logistical procedures and schedules you need to know and respect, or you'll be baking chicken and stacking chairs yourself.

Meet now so you know what you can—and can't—promise families.

## 5. Train the church receptionist

Be sure anyone who covers the church office knows what information you need should a funeral be requested. At minimum, you need to know:

- The name of the funeral home handling the funeral
- The name of the deceased
- The name of the person making the request
- The name of a contact person if it's someone other than the caller
- Several phone numbers you can use to connect with your contact person

Stress the timeliness of passing information along to you. When a family reaches out to request a funeral, they need to hear from you within hours, not days.

## 6. Consult a musician

If you're not much of a musician, ask your worship team for a list of appropriate songs you can recommend to families planning funerals.

Having that list in your pocket is a great way to avoid Cousin Darryl inviting himself to do a seven-minute cover of Led Zeppelin's *Stairway to Heaven*.

Yes, that happened. No, it wasn't pretty.

## 7. Identify funeral mentors

Especially if you find officiating funerals difficult, get to know a few pastors you can call to discuss or debrief the experience. If you're in a denomination, call your regional director. If you're on your own, who might you call on short notice to request counsel and prayer?

By doing these seven things ahead of getting the call, you'll be better prepared for when that call comes. But what do you do then? What needs to happen between that moment and the funeral service itself? Keep reading.

# 4 BEFORE THE FUNERAL

**Meet with the family point person and funeral director**

*I*f you're able to meet with the family point person and funeral director, do so—it's an opportunity to settle these details:

- When will the funeral happen?
- Where will the funeral take place?
- Who does the family want involved in the funeral service?
- Are there military or fraternal organizations to include?
- Are specific songs, readings, or Scripture passages desired?
- How long will the service last?
- Is an interpreter of some sort needed?
- Will the family return to the church building to share a meal and if so, will the church provide it?
- Are there cultural or spiritual traditions to bear in mind as you prepare a eulogy or sermon?

Also, be sure you understand what the family means by the word "funeral." You might be picturing a somber event honoring both the deceased and God—respectful and reverent. But the family may have something else in mind…like firing off cremains-loaded fireworks.

Following are several types of services that fall under the umbrella of "funeral." See which elements of these options a family wants to incorporate into their funeral experience.

A *funeral service* is formal and scripted. The remains of the deceased are present, and, following the service, mourners proceed to the graveside for a brief prayer and final farewell.

A *memorial service* remembers the loved one and may happen days or weeks after internment or cremation. Friends and family share stories, and there's often spontaneous laughter mixed in with the tears.

A *viewing* is held before the funeral service as mourners gather to see the remains of the loved one and speak with family members. There's no organized service; people come and go as they wish.

A *wake* ranges from a quiet open house to a rowdy series of toasts lifted in a bar. Some wakes are hosted by colleagues (firefighters, police, or members of the military, for instance) and don't necessarily include family members.

A *celebration of life* honors the deceased, focusing on the positive things in the person's life. It may be held at a location the deceased enjoyed and include stories, photos, and music the person liked. The emphasis is decidedly upbeat.

Don't leave a planning meeting without clearly understanding what the family expects—and deciding how you do or don't fit into the picture.

One caution: If the discussion turns to financial matters, excuse yourself and leave the family with the funeral director. In general, you don't need to be part of any conversation about the pricing of services or caskets.

## Sit down with the family

You'll also want to meet with the family to gather information for your sermon and/or eulogy. These tips will help you make the most of that meeting:

• **Meet in the family's home.** It's a more relaxed setting and helps family members connect with memories of their loved one. They may pull out photo albums or point to objects in the room to help explain a story.

• **Ask for an hour—you'll need it.** It can be therapeutic to share stories about the person who's died, so allow time for that to happen. Don't rush the family, but don't outstay your welcome, either.

• **Take notes with paper and pen, not your phone.** It will be clear you're writing down details about the deceased rather than checking the weather.

The following questions will prompt families (or, in their absence, friends) to share favorite stories about the deceased:

• What are the names of family members—spouse, children, grandkids, parents, and siblings? When you write down names, also write them phonetically so you don't mispronounce a name later.

- If this person was married, for how long?
- What was this person's work history?
- Where did this person go to school?
- What was this person's birthday, and what's the exact date of death?
- Any special accomplishments come to mind? Military or other honors?
- What was this person's church affiliation? Religious beliefs?
- What hobbies did this person enjoy?

- What was this person proud of?
- What did the person find funny?
- What stories did this person enjoy telling?
- What was important to this person?
- What did this person's friends value in him or her?
- What are a few words that describe this person's character?
- What was this person like as a child? What stories illustrate what you've said?
- Describe this person's teenage years. Stories you can share?
- Describe the young adult years.
- Describe the adult years.
- What were this person's favorite sayings?
- If this person knew death was imminent, how did he or she respond?
- What will you miss about this person?

Highlight any memory that prompts a chuckle from the family. Those are memories they'll find comforting when mentioned during the funeral.

• **Propose an outline of the service.** It's easier for grieving families to respond to an existing agenda than brainstorm one from the ground up. Share the following outline as a starting point for discussion:

1. Seating of the immediate family
2. First song
3. Greeting
4. Introduction of those who'll read the obituary and/or share stories about the deceased
5. Stories from family and friends
6. Second song
7. Scripture reading and sermon/message
8. Prayer
9. Closing remarks and instructions from the funeral director
10. Third song
11. Escorting immediate family from the room
12. Proceed to graveside service
13. Graveside service

As the outline firms up, don't let anyone cut the Scripture reading or sermon—they're your best opportunity to present the hope that's in Jesus. It may help if you refer to the sermon as a "message"—as less baggage is attached to that word.

Once the order of the funeral service is set, give the family and funeral director a copy. Agree together that should anything shift, everyone in the loop will be updated immediately.

• **Select music.** Here's where having a list of songs is useful. Offer it to the family for comment but be open to what they—or the deceased—chose for music. As possible, honor the family's requests.

Two caveats:

First, stress that music must be uplifting for mourners in attendance. A song representing a private joke ("Every Halloween Frank dressed as Tiny Tim and sang *Tiptoe Through the Tulips*—we should include it") will just confuse mourners.

Second, don't include more than a few songs. This isn't a concert; songs are best used to open and close the funeral service or as transitions between portions of the service.

If taped music will be played during the viewing or before and after the funeral service, identify that music as well. Funeral homes often have CDs or streaming playlists of appropriate instrumental music they can make available.

• **Offer to read on behalf of family members.** Family members who decide to speak during the funeral may find they're too overwhelmed in the moment to do so. Encourage speakers to write out their comments so you can step in if necessary. This offer reassures family members and encourages them to organize their thoughts.

• **Discourage an open mic situation.** Some funerals include time for anyone to stand and share stories. *Avoid this if possible.* Stories tend to ramble on at length. This time is also a platform for terrible theology as mourners declare the deceased is now an angel. On occasion, speakers have also attacked the deceased's character in an attempt to settle old scores.

If you must include an open mic session, practice the open-mic technique described in Pro Tips (Chapter 12) to minimize risk.

• **Thank the family for their hospitality.** They're both busy and hurting; their time with you is a gift.

• **Wrap up with a prayer.** Be brief but ask God to bless the family and give them peace.

## Reconnect with the funeral director

Following the family meeting, share details that impact his or her facility. A family member wants to sing a solo; are there microphones and speakers? Recorded music is desired before and after the service; how is that handled? The family wishes to screen a montage of family photos; how can that happen?

## Write the sermon and/or eulogy

Decide if you're writing a sermon or eulogy—they're not the same.

A sermon conveys Scriptural truth, focusing on God. A eulogy is an oration honoring the deceased and focuses on that individual.

Eulogies are often handled by family members, but you can count on delivering a sermon.

You'll find sample sermon outlines in Chapter 9, but the following considerations apply in all funeral sermons:

## Don't judge

Knowing the deceased knew and loved Jesus is a great relief. It's also reassuring if the person attended church or made a faith commitment in the past.

But you don't know the true condition of another person's heart. It's possible a regular church attender never knew Jesus, and a person with no formal church connection was a Christ-follower.

It's equally true you can't imply the murderer, thief, pedophile, or victim of suicide whose funeral you're officiating *isn't* in heaven. God's grace is deeper than ours, and deathbed conversions are still conversions.

The point: avoid giving reassurances about heaven or using the person who died as a cautionary tale concerning hell.

## Acknowledge the elephant in the room

If the funeral is that of a young child, a victim of suicide, or someone killed in a tragic accident, address that reality in a sensitive manner. Mourners are aware of the situation and likely need help dealing with it.

Set them on a path to peace by speaking the truth in love: Yes, the tragedy is overwhelming, but no one is alone in coping with it. God's love reaches past any tragedy and brings comfort.

### Validate mourners' pain

Nothing is gained by suggesting mourners should keep a stiff upper lip or equating sadness with a lack of faith. Instead, let mourners know their grief is both normal and an indication of how much they loved and will miss the deceased.

### Make it personal

In a eulogy, you'll use most of what you discovered while speaking to the family. If you're writing a sermon, where the focus is primarily on Christ, you can still find places where memories about the deceased are relevant.

Any sermon that fails to include comments about the deceased, as well as Jesus, will feel cold and impersonal. Just make sure you keep those two elements in proper proportion.

### Honor your time limit

However long you've agreed to speak is how long you've got—don't go a minute longer.

Some mourners won't have been in church for a very long time, if ever. What seems like a few minutes to you standing behind the podium feels far longer sitting in stackable funeral home chairs.

If you're looking for a rule of thumb regarding time, here's one: Plan a funeral service that wraps up in a half hour, taking no more than ten minutes for your message.

## Stick to your script

As a speaker, you rely on audience reaction to propel you through a talk. You tell a joke—people laugh. You share information—at least a few people make notes.

That may not happen at a funeral, where eye contact is less on you and more on the casket of the loved one. And because laughter might feel disrespectful, your attempts to lighten the mood may fall flat. You'll be tempted to abandon your prepared notes in an attempt to recapture the audience.

Don't.

Instead, go in knowing you'll move through your message with more subdued audience feedback. If you've prepared prayerfully, trust what you've brought is what should be shared.

## Fact check your sermon or eulogy

Be sure names, dates, and locations are correct. Touch base with your point of contact and quickly run through the details.

## Point to hope in Jesus

It needn't be heavy-handed, but you need to speak about Jesus because he's the only place true hope is found in the face of death.

During your meeting with the family, you'll sense how open they are to your sharing the gospel in your sermon. You may be asked not to do it at all.

Be clear you hear the request…but you need to be faithful to your calling.

Offer this: You'll mention where you find hope—that's in Jesus—but not belabor the point or ask others to make any commitment. If someone seeks you out later for a conversation, you'll share in more detail one on one.

# 5 DURING THE VIEWING

*P*eople often view the body at the funeral home the day before the funeral. You'll have to decide whether to attend and, if you do, how long to remain.

Viewings often last several hours, and it's likely the family will arrive thirty minutes before it officially begins. If possible, be there to greet them; they face a difficult few hours.

Here are several benefits to making an appearance, at least briefly:

## You'll have time with the family

In this less structured setting, it's possible to meet and speak individually with family members. You can also ask to pray for them and the mourners who'll be coming.

## You can quietly connect with the funeral director

Check to see if there's anything new you should know about the funeral.

## You can observe family dynamics

The death of loved ones brings out our best and worst, and strained relationships between relatives can hit a flashpoint. If you see conflicts escalating or conversations growing heated, you may be able to intervene and help keep the peace.

## You'll meet mourners

Introduce yourself to mourners as they filter through the room. Ask what their connection to the deceased was, how they're coping, and—if they're open to it—pray for them on the spot.

Remember, viewings are formal events. Wear dark, conservative, respectful clothing. And when the time comes for you to leave, assuming the viewing isn't yet over, let both the funeral director and your point-of-contact family member know you're departing and will see them the next day.

# 6 DURING THE FUNERAL

*H*ead into the day of a funeral spiritually attune and physically rested. You'll be in the presence of grief, and few situations require more empathy or are more emotionally demanding. And few environments provide more opportunities to do significant ministry.

Following are tips for navigating the funeral service:

**Review your role**

The funeral director will typically tell mourners where to sit and explain how and when to arrive at the graveside service, freeing you up to do what you're called to do:

- Provide comfort
- Focus on relationships
- Represent Jesus
- Serve

Before you leave home, ask God to show you how to faithfully serve him as you're present for grieving people.

**Dress for the occasion**

Wear clothing marginally more formal than you expect mourners to wear. Black clothing is best, pressed and perfect. And don't forget to shine your shoes.

How you dress will be perceived as respectful of the deceased...or not.

## Be prepared

Rehearse your sermon—especially the pronunciation of names. And review your list of family members too, so you can greet them by name.

When you're confident in your preparation, it shows. You're calm, collected, and able to engage freely with mourners. There's no need to slide off to the side to review your notes.

## Arrive early

Arrive thirty minutes before whatever time you agreed to meet the funeral director or family. Use a few of those minutes to walk through the room where mourners will gather and pray about what will happen there.

Your early arrival lets you confirm details with the funeral director, who'll undoubtedly be early as well. Has anything changed? Will weather impact how you proceed? Any last-minute suggestions?

Consider asking the funeral director to position the casket somewhere other than directly between the podium and mourners—especially if it's an open-casket funeral. It's hard for mourners to focus on what's happening behind the podium as they stare across the body of their loved one.

Position the casket slightly off-center if it still leaves room for mourners to pass by the casket.

## Double-check logistics

Are microphones working? The music stand steady and properly adjusted? Technology up and running? Funeral programs in place? The funeral director will likely have everything in hand; check in with him or her first.

Ask the funeral director about the graveside service if there will be one. Where should you stand, and how will you get to the cemetery?

Be sure the front rows of seats where the family will sit are clearly marked as reserved. Otherwise, you'll have to ask people who take those seats to move.

## Visit the family lounge

Both in a funeral home and your church building, a side room should be reserved for use by immediate family members. Be sure adequate seating and refreshments are available. This is where the family will gather as mourners filter into the room where the funeral takes place.

Join the family and provide encouragement and comfort. Just before the ceremony, ask if they will permit you to offer a prayer on their behalf.

## Take your position

Shortly before the service begins, excuse yourself from the family and take a seat in the front of the room facing the audience. Your arrival signals things are about to begin and encourages mourners to wrap up conversations and be seated.

When the family is ready to enter the room, stand and, with hand gestures, indicate mourners should stand as well. When the family is seated, signal everyone should sit and do so yourself.

## Be attentive

When a eulogy is read, a solo sung, or a poem recited, pay rapt attention. The eyes of the mourners will drift to you often; don't be caught shuffling through your notes.

And you did remember to silence your phone, yes?

## Speak with sincerity

Express your concern with tone as well as words. Be compassionate and allow that compassion to be visible.

## When you finish speaking, sit down

There may be additional music, and the funeral director will have information for the mourners.

**Stand near the casket...or not**

The family may rise and leave the room (if so, stand and indicate mourners should stand as the family exits), or they may stay to speak with mourners. The family often stands near the head of the casket to receive mourners. If they do so, stand by the foot of the casket.

As people move past, some may speak to you; most won't. If they complement your sermon, simply say "thank you." Don't engage in conversation; keep the focus on the family.

**Linger**

Once mourners are dismissed, stay near the family. This is their last opportunity to view the remains of their loved one and is often a time of intense grief.

**You may be a witness**

After mourners leave the room, the funeral director may ask you to be a witness as he or she removes jewelry from the deceased or retrieves objects previously placed in the casket. The family may have asked that certain items be placed into the casket before it's sealed too.

**Lead the casket to the hearse**

Typically, you'll precede the casket from its place in the funeral service to the hearse. When you reach the cemetery, you'll again lead the way to the graveside.

Move with somber purpose, slowly and with dignity. Don't stop to speak to anyone or otherwise impede the casket from reaching the hearse or graveside.

## Be careful graveside

Often artificial turf covers the sides of the grave. That means you won't be certain where the edge of the grave is or whether the ground is soft near the edge.

Stay a safe distance from disaster by never getting within eighteen inches of the grave.

## Keep the graveside service brief

Offer a short prayer commending the person's spirit into God's hands and read a Scripture passage. Often Psalm 23 is used.

Five minutes is about as long as you should speak.

## Make a smooth handoff if there's a military honor guard

Typically, following your brief comments, you'll step aside and the honor guard will step in. They'll fold the casket's burial flag and present it to the next of kin. Then, either live or recorded, taps will be played. In some cases, there will be one or more volleys of rifle fire.

If there's a military ceremony, when you close in prayer, thank God for the faithful service the deceased provided to his or her country.

**Clearly signal when the graveside service ends**

If you simply stop talking and stand silently, mourners will wonder if something else is coming.

Close out the time by giving instructions—invite people to pay their final respects to the deceased by approaching the casket or to express their sympathy to the grieving family. Then stand aside to make room for that to happen.

# 7 AFTER THE FUNERAL

*S*hortly after a funeral, family members quit receiving condolence cards, calls, and casseroles. And as the flurry of funeral-related activities winds down, a deep loneliness can settle in. As well as an opportunity to do ministry.

When you officiate a funeral, make a note in your calendar to do the following follow-up activities. Don't rely on memory; providing follow-up care is too important to leave it to chance.

## Send a card

Following the funeral, send hand-written cards to members of the immediate family. Express your sympathies and remind them they're loved by God and are welcome in your church. And don't settle for emails—they don't have nearly the impact.

## Make a call

Several weeks after the funeral, connect with key family members by phone. Remind them you're praying for them—offer to do that before the call ends—and provide encouragement and perspective.

## Send an encouraging faith-based book

A wide range of short, helpful books are available to assist with grieving. Several are recommended at the end of this chapter. Deliver one in person if possible; send it with a note of encouragement if a personal visit isn't an option.

## Provide referrals for grief counseling

Some people are uncomfortable initiating contact with Christian or community-based counseling resources. Your careful suggestion that such resources can be helpful may give those people permission to act. Find out what agencies and professionals offer help and have contact information available.

## Speak about the deceased

Sometimes people are hesitant to mention the deceased out of fear it will sadden the next of kin. While not every conversation should center on the deceased, give those who grieve the chance to talk about their loved ones—especially if the conversation includes fond memories.

## Pray, pray, and pray

You know the source of hope and healing, and the next of kin may not. Ask God to make himself known and for his love to be felt by the brokenhearted.

## Circle back on the first anniversary

Send a sympathy card on the anniversary of the loved one's death. It's likely the grieving hasn't ended—and your thoughtfulness will be appreciated.

## A few suggested grief resources:

*Good Grief: A Companion for Every Loss* by Granger E. Westberg (Fortress Press, 2019)

*For Those Who Hurt* by Chuck Swindoll (Zondervan, 1995)

*I Wasn't Ready to Say Goodbye: Surviving, Coping and Healing After the Sudden Death of a Loved One* by Brook Noel and Pamela Blair (Sourcebooks, 2008)

# 8 SCRIPTURES THAT COMFORT AND ENCOURAGE

## When a loved one has died

*Praise be to the God and Father of our Lord Jesus Christ, the Father of compassion and the God of all comfort, who comforts us in all our troubles, so that we can comfort those in any trouble with the comfort we ourselves receive from God.* (2 Corinthians 1: 3-4)

*The LORD is my rock, my fortress and my deliverer; my God is my rock, in whom I take refuge, my shield and the horn of my salvation. He is my stronghold, my refuge and my savior—from violent people you save me.* (2 Samuel 22:2-3)

*God is our refuge and strength, an ever-present help in times of trouble.* (Psalm 46:1)

*Praise the LORD, my soul; all my inmost being, praise his holy name. Praise the LORD, my soul, and forget not all his benefits—who forgives all your sins and heals all your diseases, who redeems your life from the pit and crowns you*

*with love and compassion, who satisfies your desires with good things so that your youth is renewed like the eagle's. The* LORD *works righteousness and justice for all the oppressed.*
(Psalm 103:1-6)

## When a believer dies

*Jesus said to her, "I am the resurrection and the life. The one who believes in me will live, even though they die; and whoever lives by believing in me will never die. Do you believe this?"*
(John 11:25-26)

*"Do not let your hearts be troubled. You believe in God; believe also in me. My Father's house has many rooms; if that were not so, would I have told you that I am going there to prepare a place for you? And if I go and prepare a place for you, I will come back and take you to be with me that you also may be where I am."*
(John 14:1-3)

*Listen, I tell you a mystery: We will not all sleep, but we will all be changed—in a flash, in the twinkling of an eye, at the last trumpet. For the trumpet will sound, the dead will be raised imperishable, and we will be changed.*

*For the perishable must clothe itself with the imperishable, and the mortal with immortality. When the perishable has been clothed with the imperishable, and the mortal with immortality, then the saying that is written will come true: "Death has been swallowed up in victory." "Where, O death, is your victory? Where, O death, is your sting?"*
(1 Corinthians 15:51-55)

*Brothers and sisters, we do not want you to be uninformed about those who sleep in death, so that you do not grieve like the rest of mankind, who have no hope. For we believe that Jesus died and rose again, and so we believe that God will bring with Jesus those who have fallen asleep in him. According to the Lord's word, we tell you that we who are still alive, who are left until the coming of the Lord, will certainly not precede those who have fallen asleep. For the Lord himself will come down from heaven, with a loud command, with the voice of the archangel and with the trumpet call of God, and the dead in Christ will rise first. After that, we who are still alive and are left will be caught up together with them in the clouds to meet the Lord in the air. And so we will be with the Lord forever. Therefore encourage one another with these words.* (1 Thessalonians 4:13-18)

*Then I saw "a new heaven and a new earth," for the first heaven and the first earth had passed away, and there was no longer any sea. I saw the Holy City, the new Jerusalem, coming down out of heaven from God, prepared as a bride beautifully dressed for her husband. And I heard a loud voice from the throne saying, "Look! God's dwelling place is now among the people, and he will dwell with them. They will be his people, and God himself will be with them and be their God. 'He will wipe every tear from their eyes. There will be no more death or mourning or crying or pain, for the old order of things has passed away." He who was seated on the throne said, "I am making everything new!" Then he said, "Write this down, for these words are trustworthy and true." He said to me: "It is done. I am the Alpha and the Omega, the Beginning and the End. To the thirsty I will give water without cost from the spring of the water of life. Those who are victorious will inherit all this, and I will be their God and they will be my children.* (Revelation 21:1-7)

*Blessed is the one who perseveres under trial because, having stood the test, that person will receive the crown of life that the Lord has promised to those who love him.* (James 1:12)

## When an unbeliever dies

*The LORD is my shepherd, I lack nothing. He makes me lie down in green pastures, he leads me beside quiet waters, he refreshes my soul. He guides me along the right paths for his name's sake. Even though I walk through the darkest valley, I will fear no evil, for you are with me; your rod and your staff, they comfort me. You prepare a table before me in the presence of my enemies. You anoint my head with oil; my cup overflows. Surely your goodness and love will follow me all the days of my life, and I will dwell in the house of the LORD forever.*
(Psalm 23)

*Praise be to the God and Father of our Lord Jesus Christ, the Father of compassion and the God of all comfort, who comforts us in all our troubles, so that we can comfort those in any trouble with the comfort we ourselves receive from God.* (2 Corinthians 1:3,4)

## When you speak of God's goodness

*The LORD is gracious and compassionate, slow to anger and rich in love. The LORD is good to all; he has compassion on all he has made.* (Psalm 145:8-9)

*Your love, LORD, reaches to the heavens, your faithfulness to the skies. Your righteousness is like the highest mountains, your justice like the great deep. You, LORD, preserve both people and animals. How priceless is your unfailing love, O God! People take refuge in the shadow of your wings.* (Psalm 36:3-7)

## When you speak to the grieving

*Who shall separate us from the love of Christ? Shall trouble or hardship or persecution or famine or nakedness or danger or sword? No, in all these things we are more than conquerors through him who loved us. For I am convinced that neither death nor life, neither angels nor demons, neither the present nor the future, nor any powers, neither height nor depth, nor anything else in all creation, will be able to separate us from the love of God that is in Christ Jesus our Lord.* (Romans 8:35, 37-39)

*Because of the LORD's great love we are not
consumed, for his compassions never fail.
they are new every morning; great is your
faithfulness.* (Lamentations 3:22-23)

*The LORD is close to the brokenhearted and
saves those who are crushed in spirit.*
(Psalm 34:18)

*"Come to me, all you who are weary and
burdened, and I will give you rest. Take my
yoke upon you and learn from me, for I am
gentle and humble in heart, and you will find
rest for your souls. For my yoke is easy and my
burden is light."* (Matthew 11:28-30)

## When you stand at a graveside

*For we know that if the earthly tent we live in
is destroyed, we have a building from God, an
eternal house in heaven, not built by human
hands. Meanwhile we groan, longing to be
clothed instead with our heavenly dwelling…
Now the one who has fashioned us for this very
purpose is God, who has given us the Spirit as a
deposit, guaranteeing what is to come. Therefore
we are always confident and know that as long
as we are at home in the body we are away from*

*the Lord. For we live by faith, not by sight.*
(2 Corinthians 5:1-2,5-7)

**Additional passages**: Isaiah 43:2-3a; Psalm 34:4-5; 7-9; Psalm 91:1-4; 2 Corinthians 4:7-12.

# 9 SAMPLE SERMONS

*U*se these general templates as starting points for your own sermons. They're thin on details because you'll need to provide those yourself.

Notice each sermon outline includes information about the deceased and points to hope in Jesus.

**A basic sermon**

1. Introduction (if you've not already been introduced).

2. Explain you've been with the deceased's family and now know the deceased better through their stories about him.

3. Share touching memories the family shared with you.

4. Describe the positive qualities you discovered about the deceased through the stories.

5. Say: "Today, we feel the loss of (the deceased), and I know that nothing I can say will ease your pain. But I know words that do heal—they're the words of God found in Scripture. I'd like to read a few of them now..."

6. Read 1 Thessalonians 4:13-18 and Lamentations 3:22-23.

7. Say: "And here are reassuring words for us today..."

8.  Read Psalm 34:18.

9.  Close in prayer.

## A sermon for an infant or child

1.  Introduction (if you've not already been introduced)

2.  Say: "Today is a tragic day. No words can describe the pain of losing a child; no hugs can sweep that pain from one's heart. That's true for the family of (the deceased) today, and true for the rest of us too."

3.  Say: "(The deceased's) life was young—but not small. I say that because it was a life overflowing with love."

4.  Explain (the deceased) was loved by her parents, her grandparents—name them—and by other family and friends. Describe how that love was shown. Describe how loving (the deceased) was.

5.  Say: "We're gathered here as a witness to this young life and to be with those who grieve its loss. (The deceased) did not leave this world unnoticed. Not by us—and not by God."

6.  Read John 14:1-3.

7.  Say: "I believe (the deceased) is in the shelter of God's arms. And it's my hope that we'll all

one day be together there with (the deceased).
For now, know this: God has not forgotten
you either."

8. Read Psalm 34:18.

9. Close in prayer.

## A sermon for a victim of suicide or a person who dies unexpectedly

1. Introduction (if you've not already been introduced).

2. Explain you've been with the deceased's family. Say: "They—like you—have felt overwhelmed and shattered. Many tears have been shed...and more will come. That's true for us all as we cope with the loss of (loved one)."

3. Share that you know the deceased better through the family's stories about him.

4. Share touching memories the family shared.

5. Describe the positive qualities you discovered about the deceased through the stories.

6. Say: "Many of us sit here today with a question echoing in our minds: 'Why?' I don't have the answer...nor do you. But I do have this..."

7. Read Psalm 145:8-9. Say: "I know that (the deceased) was loved—by you and also by

God. I know that God loves (the deceased)
still, and it's my prayer that (the deceased) may
be experiencing the fullness of that love. I
pray the same for all of us."

8.  Close in prayer.

## A sermon for someone whose death was caused by another person

1.  Introduction (if you've not already been
    introduced).

2.  Say: "And here we are, gathered to mourn
    the loss of (the deceased). Some of us have
    lost a son/daughter, a nephew/niece, a
    brother/sister. Some of us have lost a friend,
    a classmate, a colleague. And all of us sit with
    the certainty that this tragedy should not have
    happened…that this is *not* a place we should
    be."

3.  Admit you share in the sadness and anger and
    you, too, wonder at the injustice.

4.  Say: "I won't stand here and attempt to
    comfort you with platitudes about how this
    death was all part of God's plan or that
    everything—no matter how hard—works
    for the good. Even if those things are true,
    they're not comforting. Not now. Not when
    our hearts cry for justice and we're hollowed

out with grief. But I will tell you about the
treasure that's been snatched away from us."

5. Explain you've spoken with the family and
   learned more about the deceased.

6. Share touching memories the family shared.

7. Describe positive qualities about the deceased
   you discovered through the stories.

8. Say: "You'll miss (the deceased), but know this:
   even in this hard time, there's hope—because
   while (the deceased) is no longer with us, his
   life hasn't ended. The Bible tells us this…"

9. Read Romans 8:35, 37-39.

10. Say: "As we feel the depths of our grief, let's
    also be touched by the hope found in Jesus.
    Today is not the end of (the deceased's) story.
    He's with the God who loves him, a place we
    can one day be as well. All is not lost, and all
    is not over."

11. Close in prayer.

## A sermon for a public figure

*Expect a large and diverse audience at this funeral*

1. Introduction (if you've not already been
   introduced)

2. Say: "Some people seem to be a little larger
   than others. Their accomplishments and

commitment to service set them apart. (The deceased) was one of those people."

3. Read the eulogy or highlight some of the public figure's accomplishments.

4. Say: "That's a life that had impact. Impact on this community and perhaps in your own lives. (The deceased) certainly had an impact on his family."

5. Share some memories you heard from family members.

6. Say: "Today, the impact we feel from (the deceased) is his absence. Some of you have lost a close friend...a beloved family member...a valued colleague. But we aren't left with just the pain of this absence—we can also have hope."

7. Read Romans 8:35, 37-39, emphasizing "*death*."

8. Say: "The love of God reached out to (the deceased) and reaches out to us. In it, we still feel the absence of (the deceased), but we also experience hope. Hope that can heal, hope that provides a promise. I choose to embrace that hope, and perhaps you do too.

9. Close in prayer.

## A sermon for a teenager or young adult

1. Introduction (if you've not already been introduced).

2. Say: "Some have said that your life is measured not just by the years you live, but by the living you do in the years you're given. By that measure (the deceased) had a longer life than many."

3. Explain you've been with (the deceased's) family and now know (the deceased) better because of stories shared about the living (the deceased).

4. Describe the deceased's activities and accomplishments as touching memories the family shared.

5. Describe positive qualities about the deceased you discovered through stories.

6. Say: "None of that takes away the pain we feel at the loss of (the deceased). Or answers the question, 'Why?' Why was (the deceased) taken at so young an age? Why are his/her parent(s) and family enduring a pain so deep it feels like it can't be endured: the loss of a child?"

7. Say: "I have no answer to that question. Nor do you. And I'm certain no answer anyone could give would satisfy. That question comes

from the depth of our pain, and today, I want to honor our pain and grief. It's real… and we feel what we feel. But I do have this for you: hope. Hope in the God who loved (the deceased) just as deeply as you love (the deceased). Scripture tells us this…"

8. Read Romans 8:35, 37-39.

9. Say: I find hope in that passage. Hope for (the deceased) and hope for us. Hope that the love of God is embracing (the deceased), and that the same love will give us peace in the long days ahead. The Psalmist wrote…"

10. Read Psalm 34:18

11. Say: "It seems the Psalmist was writing about…us."

12. Close in prayer.

## A sermon for someone who suffered a long-term illness

1. Introduction (if you've not already been introduced).

2. Say: "Throughout the years, I've had this question posed to me several times: Would I rather know when my death is imminent or die suddenly with no advance notice? For (the deceased), his long-term illness answered that

question for him. He knew death was knocking at his door. He had time to prepare—and to consider what death would take from him."

3. Explain you've spent time with his family and have discovered the rich life the deceased led.

4. Outline the deceased's family, friends, and passions in life. Describe what and who he loved and why he was loved by those around him.

5. Say: "That's a lot to lose, and (the deceased) wasn't eager to lose it. Nor were those who loved him eager to lose (the deceased). But (the deceased) knew something that took the sting from that loss—that brought him hope and comfort. The Bible says this…"

6. Read aloud Romans 8:35, 37-3

7. Say: "(The deceased) knew what we can know: death isn't the end. Nothing can separate us from the love of God, and that love—the redeeming, death-defying love found in Jesus—carries those who know him beyond the grave. I look forward to being with (the deceased) again in the place Jesus has prepared for (the deceased). Because I'm invited too—as are you."

8. Close in prayer.

**A sermon for a believer you don't know**

1. Introduction (if you've not already been introduced)

2. Share the birth and death dates, where the deceased was born, and where he died.

3. Say: "Those are the facts, but facts don't sum up a life well-lived. It's what happened between those dates that tell the story, and there were plenty of stories in the life of (the deceased)."

4. Share touching memories the family shared of the deceased. Describe what the deceased enjoyed doing (use your research) and what those activities said about the character of the deceased.

5. Say: "Part of (the deceased's) story was another story—one that brought meaning and hope. It's a story (the deceased) embraced wholeheartedly."

6. Read John 11:25-2

7. Say: "(The deceased) answered Jesus' question with a 'yes,' and that's why I look forward to one day meeting (the deceased)—in heaven. It's my hope we'll all be together there."

8. Close in prayer

## A sermon for a believer you know

1. Introduction (if you've not already been introduced).

2. Share with mourners you're grieving too (*describe your relationship with the deceased*).

3. Explain what you had in common with the deceased, including faith in Jesus.

4. Share what you didn't have in common—unique things about the deceased.

5. Share touching memories you or the family have of the deceased.

6. Say: "Carved on tombstones is a date for both birth and death, but what matters more is what happens between those dates. (The deceased) filled much of that space with following Jesus and, as a result, could look with confidence at a future that stretches far beyond that final date."

7. Read Revelation 21:1-7

8. Say: "I look forward to joining (the deceased) in that place—and I hope all of us will be part of that joyful reunion with (the deceased)."

9. Close in prayer

## A sermon for a fallen soldier

*Adapt this sermon for a fallen first responder*

1. Introduction (if you've not already been introduced)

2. Say: "(The deceased) was many things to many people—friend, son, father, and brother among them. But he died a soldier; he died serving his country. The Bible is full of soldiers, but none surpasses the soldier who became king: David. A psalm often read at times like this is Psalm 23—a psalm written by David.

3. Read Psalm 23.

4. Point out that in the psalm, the shepherd is described as caring for his sheep the way a military leader cares for his troops. The deceased cared for people in his life—give several examples from his family.

5. The shepherd provides for his flock. Give an example of how the deceased met the needs of those he loved.

6. The shepherd protects his flock. The deceased fought to protect those he loved and his country.

7. The shepherd inspired his flock to have courage, to carry on.

8. Say: "(The deceased) carried on—on into service, to battle, to give the ultimate sacrifice. We, like the deceased, have a shepherd too. One who cares for us, who fights for us, who

loves and leads us. His name is Jesus, and at moments like these, he gently offers us not just strength, but comfort."

9. Read Lamentations 3:22-23

10. Close in prayer.

## A celebration of life sermon

*This service is typically less structured than most funerals; expect spontaneous sharing*

1. Introduction (if you've not already been introduced)

2. Say: "Jesus was explaining to some religious leaders why he'd come and what he had in mind for those who followed him. He said this…"

3. Read John 10:10b.

4. Say: "A rich and satisfying life—that's what we celebrate today as we remember (the deceased). Today, there may be tears, laughter, or both—because a rich life holds both in abundance."

5. Invite people who've agreed to share stories about the deceased to do so.

6. Present any video tribute and play any music the family wishes to share.

7. Describe positive attributes of the deceased and how they contributed to a rich and satisfying life.

8. Say: "The religious leaders talking with Jesus didn't fully understand who he was. They didn't realize knowing him was the key to living a rich and fulfilling life. (The deceased) knew that, and it's one reason I believe we're celebrating a life that has not yet ended. The Bible says this…"

9. Read John 11:25-26.

10. Say: "(The deceased) answered that question with a 'yes,' and his answer fueled his rich and fulfilling life. I've got to believe the same answer will do the same for you."

11. Close in prayer.

## Graveside remarks for a believer

*Keep your comments brief—and focused on Jesus.*

1. Say: "There's no more solemn moment than this: standing beside the grave of someone we love. But we're saying goodbye not to (the deceased) but to a body (the deceased) no longer needs."

2. Read aloud 2 Corinthians 5:1-2, 5-7.

3. Say: "As we commit the body of (the deceased)

to the ground, we live in the hope and certainty of resurrection, of one day being reunited with (the deceased). Pray with me."

4. Pray, committing the deceased's body to the ground and his spirit to God.

# 10 PRAYERS TO SHARE

*T*he most meaningful prayers are heartfelt and personal. Before praying for mourners, pause to ask God how he'd have you pray for them. God knows their hearts—and pain.

Here are a few general prayers but know that your sincere prayers in the moment will almost certainly be more comforting to those who hear them.

*Dear God,*

*You made (the deceased) in your image, designing him for eternity. We're grateful for the years we had with (the deceased) and know he's now in your care, loved and embraced as your child. Comfort us in our loss and guide us as we move forward.*

*Amen.*

*God,*

*You are light and life, and we praise you for who you are. Guide us with your light and fill us with your life as we mourn the loss of (the deceased). We rest in knowing he is now with you, but we miss him, God. Be with us.*

*Amen.*

*Dear God,*

*We ask for healing. Our hearts are bruised with the loss of (the deceased). In the days ahead, be with us, and bring to mind memories of how you enriched our lives through (the deceased). We pray for joy to rise up in us again, God, as it rises with (the deceased) as he's with you.*

*Amen.*

*God,*

*Be with the family of (the deceased). They're learning to live with an empty place at the table, a silence where there was once laughter. Fill their hearts with love, God, and remind them always that you are with them, that they're not alone.*

*Amen.*

*Dear God,*

*We know that (the deceased) is now with you, standing in your presence in a place swept clean of pain and tears. But we're not there yet, God, and feel the sting of our loss. We taste the salt of our tears. Give us joy in you. Remind us of your love and help us feel it.*

*Amen.*

# 11 SELF-CARE

*Y*ou're best able to serve others when you're healthy spiritually, emotionally, and physically. Here are ways to care for yourself as you shoulder the challenges of officiating funerals.

## Monitor your emotions

As you help others cope with the death of a loved one, you may find you're reacting to the intensity of the experience.

The question is: how much are you reacting?

It's hard to accurately evaluate our own emotional well-being, so ask a spouse or close friend if they see changes in you when you're dealing with funerals and grief. Are you increasingly sad or distant? Quick to grow angry or snap at others?

Dealing with death may churn up feelings of loss or pain from our own pasts. We're sideswiped by emotion, surprised at the intensity of our reactions.

If that's true for you, get help dealing with whatever fuels your strong responses. Not only will you be healthier, but you'll also be better prepared to provide comfort to others.

## Get it out

Don't let the stress that comes with confronting death simmer under the surface. Frank conversations, honest prayers, and even workout sessions at the gym can all help you cope.

## Set boundaries...and keep them

Set boundaries that protect you and the stability of your emotions and life. Be available to grieving people, but don't let stress and grief erode your health, family life, or ability to perform other pastoral duties.

It's okay to tell grieving family members you're available during specific hours or that you can't meet with them at certain times. Be available, but not necessarily on call.

Remember, your kids still need to be tucked in. And the rest of the congregation still expects a sermon this Sunday.

## Care for yourself physically

Exercise, sufficient sleep, and an intentionally healthy diet all provide the energy you need to be effective during emotionally challenging times.

## Care for yourself relationally

If a funeral forced you to cancel lunch dates with friends or walks with a spouse, get those rescheduled as soon as possible. You need them, and they matter.

## Care for yourself spiritually

Facing the reality of death puts our beliefs about eternal life, God's goodness, and the sufficiency of grace to the test. When a drunk driver kills a family of four on their way to church, can we honestly say God is good? When sudden infant death syndrome claims the life of a months-old baby, how sure are you God has a plan?

If you find yourself questioning truths you've never questioned in the past, seek out a mentor and together embrace those questions.

Don't duck them—you're growing stronger in your faith.

## Don't take it personally

Grief-stricken people sometimes lash out, infuriated with God for not saving their loved one or at least explaining why she died. As a church leader, the anger they feel for God may be redirected your way.

It's not personal. And they aren't ready for a calm conversation or for you to open a Bible to help them understand what can be understood.

That's later when you follow up in a week and say, "You raised a question and I've given it some thought. Can I have twenty minutes to attempt to answer it?"

But standing by the casket isn't the place or time.

# 12 PRO TIPS

**Back everything up**

*Y*our sermon, the eulogy, the order of service, readings, any music that will be played—have several copies on the day of the funeral. Someone will forget to bring what they need, and you'll be ready to help.

**If you're co-officiating with another church leader, coordinate messages**

Make sure you're not using the same scripture passages or covering identical ground in your sermons.

And don't be offended if a family asks someone else to also officiate. Including another pastor isn't an indication you're not trusted; it's a reminder the family has been blessed to have more than one spiritual advisor in their lives.

**Gather close**

If the funeral home has arranged a tent shelter over the grave, mourners tend to stand outside rather than under it. Invite them in closer when you start to speak. It will be easier for everyone to hear you and to feel a part of the service.

## Remember who's in charge

When you're in a funeral home, the funeral director is in charge. If a decision needs to be made or a change considered, involve the funeral director rather than forging ahead on your own.

## If someone is under the influence

More than once, family members or mourners have shown up at viewings or funerals fortified with alcohol or drugs. If someone is under the influence and becoming disruptive, enlist the funeral director's help in calling the individual out of the room. Don't let anyone hijack the funeral with disruptive behavior.

## Bring tape

At the graveside service, tape your notes inside your Bible so no stray gust of wind can carry them away.

## Have an umbrella handy

Even if the weather report says "sunny," have a large umbrella (so the funeral director can hold it over both of you) available. You'll be able to continue at the graveside even if rain blows in.

## Honorariums

Don't expect to be paid, but an honorarium is often presented to pastors who handle funerals. If you're paid, graciously thank the family. If you're not paid, remember Jesus didn't get renumerated for resurrecting Lazarus either (and that was *far* more impressive than what you've done).

### Attend anyway

Don't attend only funerals you officiate. If someone in your congregation or neighborhood dies, attending their funeral shows church members and neighbors you care.

### Buy a funeral outfit

Get a good black suit or dress. You'll use it for funerals, weddings, and other formal occasions. Keep it clean, pressed, and at the ready.

### Never complain

Even if the need for a funeral comes at the least convenient time for you, never indicate to the family of the deceased that it's bad timing.

### Identify your place in the procession

Find out from the funeral director how you'll get to the cemetery for the graveside service. It's common for the family to be directly behind the hearse and for your car to follow the family—but not always. Don't get caught running around the parking lot trying to get instructions or hitch a ride.

### Circle back

A few days after the funeral, circle back to debrief with the funeral director. How did it go from her perspective? Does she have any advice for you? Did you think the funeral director did anything especially helpful or meaningful?

### Remember: You can always say no.

If you're asked to compromise your beliefs or told you absolutely can't mention God or Jesus, you might want to respectfully pass on doing the funeral.

You have that right—but don't do it without offering an explanation as to your reasons. Do what you can to accommodate family requests, but don't betray your calling or let yourself be used.

Your dignity isn't worth much, but your integrity is.

### Bend when possible

Not every element of the funeral is equally important. So long as you present the gospel, do you really care if someone reads a poem that's questionable in its theology? If you're asked to read something you can't endorse, it's fine to say, "I was given this to read by our friend's family," before reading.

You've distanced yourself and still served the family.

## Be generous about corrections

Sooner or later, someone at a funeral will tell you the deceased is now an angel, or that heaven is on Mars, or…well, you get the idea.

Be generous with corrections. The funeral isn't a place to have extended theological conversations. If the mistakes don't stand in the way of someone understanding the gospel, let things slide.

## Never surrender the microphone

If there's an open mic time during the funeral, either have those who wish to share join you in the front or carry a handheld microphone to them. Do *not* hand the microphone to the speaker; instead, hold it in front of the person. They'll attempt to take it from you but smile as you insist on holding it and invite the speaker to begin sharing.

This posture lets you control when to cut off the speaker by gently squeezing the person's arm and then thanking the person for sharing and asking who else has something to say.

Thank you for carrying out this important ministry to those mourning the loss of a loved one. As you venture forward in faith, may the grace and peace of the Lord be with you.

## About the Contributors

### Author

*Mikal Keefer* is a Christian writer who has written more than 40 books and has contributed to a wide array of magazines and curricula. Through his personal ministry experience and interviews with dozens of pastors far and wide, he serves up valuable and useful information in an approachable way and always with a side of good humor.

### General Editor

*Matthew Lockhart* spent more than twenty-five years serving in a variety of editorial and leadership roles in Christian publishing at Serendipity House, Group, and Standard/David C. Cook. With a penchant for book series development, he enjoys helping to create Kingdom-focused resources like the *ChurchLeaders Pastoral Pocket Guides*.

**Special thanks** to the pastors who shared their collective wisdom and insights to help make this practical pastoral guide possible.